Poles in Michigan

Dennis Badaczewski

Michigan State University Press

East Lansing

♾ The paper used in this publication meets the minimum requirements
of ANSI/NISO Z39.48-1992 (R 1997) (Permanence of Paper)

Michigan State University Press
East Lansing, Michigan 48823-5202

Printed and bound in the United States of America

08 07 06 05   2 3 4 5 6 7 8 9 10

LIBRARY OF CONGRESS CATALOGING-IN-PUBLICATION DATA
Badaczewski, Dennis, 1943–
Poles in Michigan / Dennis Badaczewski.
p. cm. — (Discovering the peoples of Michigan)
Includes bibliographical references and index.
ISBN 0-87013-618-6 (Paper : alk. paper)
1. Polish Americans—Michigan—History. 2. Polish
Americans—Michigan—Social conditions. 3.
Immigrants—Michigan—History. 4. Michigan—Ethnic relations. 5.
Michigan—Social conditions. I. Title. II. Series.
F575.P7 B33 2002
977.4'00491851—dc21
2001007958

Discovering the Peoples of Michigan. The editors wish
to thank the Kellogg Foundation for their generous support.

Cover design by Ariana Grabec-Dingman
Book design by Sharp Des!gns, Inc.

COVER PHOTO: Pazcki Day in Hamtramck, courtesy
of *The Citizen* (Hamtramck, Mich.)

Visit Michigan State University Press on the World Wide Web at:
www.msupress.msu.edu

Poles in Michigan

DISCOVERING THE PEOPLES OF MICHIGAN
Arthur W. Helweg and Linwood H. Cousins, Series Editors

Ethnicity in Michigan: Issues and People
Jack Glazier, Arthur W. Helweg

French Canadians in Michigan
John P. DuLong

African Americans in Michigan
Lewis Walker, Benjamin C. Wilson, Linwood H. Cousins

Albanians in Michigan
Frances Trix

Jews in Michigan
Judith Levin Cantor

Amish in Michigan
Gertrude Enders Huntington

Italians in Michigan
Russell M. Magnaghi

Germans in Michigan
Jeremy W. Kilar

Poles in Michigan
Dennis Badaczewski

Dutch in Michigan
Larry ten Harmsel

Asian Indians in Michigan
Arthur W. Helweg

Discovering the Peoples of Michigan is a series of publications examining the state's rich multicultural heritage. The series makes available an interesting, affordable, and varied collection of books that enables students and lay readers to explore Michigan's ethnic dynamics. A knowledge of the state's rapidly changing multicultural history has far-reaching implications for human relations, education, public policy, and planning. We believe that Discovering the Peoples of Michigan will enhance understanding of the unique contributions that diverse and often unrecognized communities have made to Michigan's history and culture.

To my late parents, Stanley Badaczewski
and Rita Gorecki Badaczewski,
who made me proud of being Polish
and American; and to my sons
Dennis and Donald, who carry on that pride.

ACKNOWLEDGMENTS

Donald Badaczewski, my brother and authority on all things Polish, opened many doors for me. My wife Sandra Michaels provided personal and editorial support. Arthur Helweg, series co-editor, and Elizabeth Demers, senior editor at Michigan State University Press, provided insightful assistance at all stages of this project. Russ Magnaghi served as a valuable historical resource and Kristy Jo Masse brought me into the twenty-first century with her research assistance. Finally, the late Peter Slavchef, who began this project.

SERIES ACKNOWLEDGMENTS

Discovering the Peoples of Michigan is a series of publications that resulted from the cooperation and effort of many individuals. The people recognized here are not a complete representation, for the list of contributors is too numerous to mention. However, credit must be given to Jeffrey Bonevich, who worked tirelessly with me on contacting people as well as researching and organizing material.

The initial idea for this project came from Mary Erwin, but I must thank Fred Bohm, director of the Michigan State University Press, for seeing the need for this project, for giving it his strong support, and for making publication possible. Also, the tireless efforts of Keith Widder and Elizabeth Demers, senior editors at Michigan State University Press were vital in bringing DPOM to fruition. Keith put his heart and soul into this series, and his dedication was instrumental in its success.

Otto Feinstein and Germaine Strobel of the Michigan Ethnic Heritage Studies Center patiently and willingly provided names for contributors and constantly gave this project their tireless support.

My late wife, Usha Mehta Helweg, was the initial editor. She meticulously went over manuscripts. Her suggestions and advice were crucial. Initial typing, editing, and formatting were also done by Majda Seuss, Priya Helweg, and Carol Nickolai.

Many of the maps in the series were drawn by Fritz Seegers while the graphics showing ethnic residential patterns in Michigan were done by the Geographical Information Center (GIS) at Western Michigan University under the directorship of David Dickason. Additional maps have been contributed by Ellen White.

Russell Magnaghi must also be given special recognition for his willingness to do much more than be a contributor. He provided author contacts as well as information to the series' writers. Other authors and organizations provided comments on other aspects of the work. There are many people that were interviewed by the various authors who will remain anonymous. However, they have enabled the story of their group to be told. Unfortunately, their names are not available, but we are grateful for their cooperation.

Most of all, this work is a tribute to the writers who patiently gave their time to write and share their research findings. Their contributions are noted and appreciated. To them goes most of the gratitude.

ARTHUR W. HELWEG, *Series Co-editor*

Contents

Poles in Michigan

Trying to discover the culture of a group as diverse as the Polish Americans is a challenge for anyone. A common theme, however, is that Poles have been proud of being hyphenated Americans since their arrival in this country, and the Poles in Michigan have followed this pattern. This small volume examines immigration patterns, internal migration, social and cultural characteristics, and the Poles as members in society at large. The richness of the Polish experience in Michigan comes to life through the many stories, cultural artifacts, and data presented.

On 30 July 1619, six Polish artisans—Michal Lowicki, Zbigniew Stefanski, Jur Mata, Jan Bogdan, Karol Zrenica and Stanislaw Sadowski—launched the first labor walkout in America at Jamestown, Virginia. The strike was not over wages or working conditions, but voting rights. The first legislature in America, the Virginia House of Burgesses did not allow them the same voting privileges as English settlers.[1] The strike by these skilled craftsmen who came to Jamestown in 1608 to establish a glass works, a tar and pitch distillery, and a soap works ended when they were allowed to vote. By their actions they expressed attitudes typical of most Polish Americans: a deep love of freedom and a willingness to fight for it.

Poles have been in America since the beginning of European immigration, arriving twelve years before *The Mayflower* landed at Plymouth Rock. Some believe that Jan Kolno, a Polish explorer who worked for Christian I of Denmark, piloted a fleet of Danish ships that touched the coast of Labrador and sailed down the Delaware River in 1476, sixteen years before Columbus mistakenly landed in the Bahamas.[2] Others believe that Francis Warnadowicz, identified by the Spanish name Francis Fernandez was a member of Columbus' crew and was the first European killed in the New World. The Jamestown Poles are well documented and a memorial to them exists at the Jamestown historical site.[3]

Early Poles in Michigan

In 1762 the marriage of Francis and Genevieve Godek was recorded in St. Anne's Church the oldest Catholic parish in Detroit.[4] They are the first Poles officially listed as residents of Michigan, but little more is known of them. The first Polish quarter or neighborhood in Michigan was in Muskegon in the 1830s. The first Polish settlement was in Huron County at Parisville near Port Huron. We know that five Poles, Francis Susala, Anton Slavik, Francis Polle, Thomas Smielewski, and Ambrose Smielewski purchased land from the federal government in 1856 and established Paris Township. They migrated from Canada, probably crossing the St. Clair River to established Polish farms.[5]

The Parisville settlement was only the second Polish settlement in America, being preceded by the Panna Maria settlement in Texas established by a Catholic priest, Father Leopold Moczygemba, in 1854. The second oldest Polish settlement in Michigan was started in 1870 in Alpena County by Poles from the province of Posen, Poland. While the Parisville settlement has virtually disappeared Posen, the German spelling of the Polish province of Poznan, continues to exist.

These early settlements were rural, but the majority of Michigan Poles now live in urban and suburban areas. In 1860 the United States had a population of 31.5 million of which 30,000 were Poles. Fifty years later, in 1910, the Polish population had increased 100 times to 3 million. The growth of the Polish population in the United States corresponded with the expansion of industry. This growth in the number of Poles is

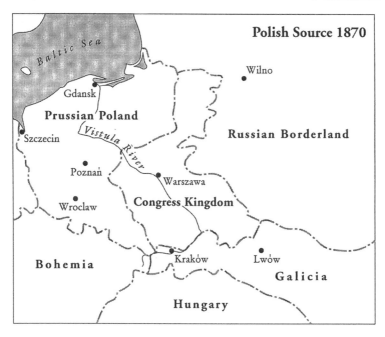

Figure 1. Polish Source Map, 1870.

best understood by a look at political and economic factors in Poland during that time.[6] Being Polish is as much an idea as it is a fact. When most of the people who identify themselves as Poles came to this country, Poland did not exist as a governmental unit. In 1770 Poland was the third largest country in Europe with an area of 280,000 square miles (about five times as large as Michigan) and fifth in population with 11.5 million people. Blessed with fertile soil, but lacking any real natural borders, Poland was a tempting target to more affluent neighbors. The country was partitioned and apportioned three times in a short period; to Russia in 1792, to Prussia in 1793, and to Austria in 1795.[7] Consequently, immigrants who considered themselves Polish were often identified by U.S. immigration officials as Russian, Prussian, or Austrian.

The first Poles to come to America were often nobles who had lost their titles. The American Revolutionary War heroes Tadeuz Kosciuszko and Casimir Pulaski were both exiled from Poland for resisting the dismemberment of their homeland. Those who stayed tried to reunite Poland. The unsuccessful insurrections of 1831, 1848, and 1863 led to many soldiers immigrating to America. The first small cohort of Poles in Michigan and America were political refugees. The majority of Polish immigrants to the United States and Michigan came in three distinct waves. The first and largest wave, between 1880 and 1920, sought employment opportunities in the automobile industry. They were different than the earlier travelers in that they were mainly farmers, artisans, and traders who had few economic opportunities in a partitioned Poland. In 1882 there were about 1,200 Poles in Detroit; by 1892 there were 35,000. Most worked at industrial jobs in the city. By 1900 nearly all of the 3,000 workers at the Peninsular Car Company, a manufacturer of railroad cars, in Detroit were Polish born. By 1915 most of Detroit's cigars were made by unskilled Polish born women and girls, many quite young. Over 7,000, including my thirteen-year-old maternal grandmother Antoinette Zielinski, worked in one of the ten largest cigar factories. In 1916 the largest ethnic group working at the Ford Motor Company were Poles. They represented 7,525 of 40,906 employees.[8]

Census figures from 1900 reported that 383,407 Poles lived in America—39% from Prussian Poland, 40% from Russian Poland, and 15% from Austrian Poland. A decade later there were 875,000 Poles in the United States. The peak year for Polish immigration was 1912, when 174,365 entered. In 1930 almost 25% of the Poles in America, 300,870 of 1,268,583, lived in Detroit. The total number of people of Polish stock (one or two Polish parents) was 3,342,198.[9]

World War I temporarily ended European immigration. After the war, Poland was once again an independent, though smaller, country. Over 250,000 Poles living in America returned to Poland. Many of these were from the 28,000 volunteer soldiers who joined a Polish American division that fought alongside Polish forces in Europe. In 1920 the federal Johnson-Reed Act established a quota system for immigrants and severely limited the number of Poles who could immigrate to the United States.[10]

The second wave of Polish immigrants came after World War II. In 1945 Poland became, politically, part of the Union of Soviet Socialist

Republics and was essentially governed from Moscow. The refugees or displaced persons, pejoratively referred to as "DP"s, were called the *nowa emigracia*, or new immigrants. Over 200,000 came to the United States, and 38,000 of them came to Michigan. As opposed to the earlier immigrants, they were more likely to have been educated urban dwellers who were often resented by less urbane earlier Poles.[11]

The third wave of immigration was from 1965 to 1992, and consisted of quota immigrants, refugees, and non-immigrants on temporary visas. From 1965 to 1990 there were 88,365 immigrants and 42,827 political refugees who arrived from Poland. Many of these new arrivals were supporters of the Solidarity movement in Poland. By far the largest group of new arrivals were the *wakacjusze* (vacationers) who totaled 666,946 by 1990. Many of these vacationers came on temporary visas but stayed and became part of the underground economy working at cash jobs that avoided any record keeping. Of the third wave, 34% were professionals, 27% were skilled workers, and only 7% had formerly worked at low paying service jobs in Poland.[12]

A fourth wave of Polish immigrants may now be in progress. In 1992, recognizing the number of vacationers not returning to Poland, the American government established a lottery system to allow visitors permanent status. In many cases those on temporary visas were males who came to Detroit and other places to work, save money, and return home with their savings. They often lived with three or four others in the same situation and were able to live frugally. Several have been able to come to the United States temporarily while their families applied for entry under the lottery system. If successful they returned to Poland and brought their families to America.

Outstate Polish Settlements

Poles are the second largest immigrant ethnic group in Michigan. This is reflected in their presence throughout the state. Grand Rapids, Michigan's second largest city, also has the second largest contingent of Poles.

The Grand Rapids area has over 300,000 people. The largest ethnic group, Dutch from the Netherlands, began arriving in groups in 1846.

The first Pole, Joseph Jakubowicz (later changed to Jackoboice) arrived alone in 1853. By 1869 about a dozen immigrants including the families of Joseph Jakubowicz, Anthony Stiller, Jacob Pogodzinski, Simon Dzieniszewski, Andrew Poposki, Stanislaw Cerklewski, Thomas Kolczynski, Albert Damski, Francis Tloczynski, and John Lipczynski, all came from the Poznan area of German Poland, as did the early settlers in Posen. Most of these settlers were skilled craftsmen who worked as shoemakers, tailors, blacksmiths, carpenters, cabinet makers, and wagon makers.

By 1882 there were enough Polish families in Grand Rapids to build a Catholic church named after St. Adalbert, the patron saint of Poland. Soon there were over two hundred Polish families living on the west side of Grand Rapids. Another neighborhood began on the northeast side of town and a third in the southwest. The latter group came to work in the large gypsum mines in the area. Most were unskilled laborers from Austrian and Russian Poland.

The early Polish community in Grand Rapids was both large and active. The first Polish Hall of the largest national Polish organization, the Polish National Alliance, was dedicated in Grand Rapids in 1899. There also was a local Polish newspaper, the *Echo Tygodnjowe* (*Weekly Echo*), published from 1900 to 1957.[13]

Few Michiganians are aware that Michigan had extensive coalmines and that they employed many Polish and Italian immigrants. The last mine, the Swan Creek Mine, closed in 1952. Theodore "Pete" Wend was one of the last of the Polish miners in Michigan. In an interview conducted in 1984 when he was 91, Pete spoke of the mines southwest of Saginaw. His parents had followed a typical immigration pattern, going to the Pennsylvania coalmines in the 1880s from Poland and relocating to St. Charles, Michigan, in the 1890s. Pete was the president of the miner's union at the Swan Creek Mine when it closed in 1952. The coalmining museum in St. Charles has a statue of Pete and his brother.[14]

Ninety-four separate Polish parochial communities in Michigan, forty-one in the Detroit area, and fifty-three outstate, are a good indicator of where Polish immigrants settled. The earliest newcomers in Parisville in the Thumb area, and Posen near Alpena, were mainly farmers. Other sizable settlements in the Thumb were at Port Austin and

Figure 2. Polish settlements and family clusters in Polonian Settlements in Michigan.

Ubly where parishes were established in 1869 and 1885 respectively. The growing shipping trade on the Great Lakes also provided ample employment. Later settlements in Kinde (1903) and Rapson (1912) were populated by former Polish farmers who migrated from urban centers.

The area around Alpena in northeast Michigan had six substantial Polish communities all established near the end of the nineteenth century. Posen was the first but was quickly followed by Rogers City, Alpena, Cheboygan, Mullet Lake, and Metz.[15] Rogers City and Alpena had mines and were also ports while Cheboygan had a paper mill and shipped paper products. Mullet Lake (Riggsville) and Metz were lumbering and farming settlements. In the 1870s about two hundred Polish families lived south of Bay City and worked in the local sugar beet fields.

With the expansion of logging opportunities the Poles found jobs at better wages in the lumber mills. By 1900, Bay City had the largest concentration of Poles outside of Detroit.[16]

Today, with very few Polish enclaves in cities, suburbs, or rural areas Poles live most everywhere in Michigan. Original settlers, however, looked for friendly faces in a new land and often settled in areas with other Poles. Searches of census data can locate areas where Poles lived in Michigan while searches of archdiocesan records can locate Catholic parishes that were recognized as Polish.

The southernmost Polish settlement was in Bronson, just north of the Indiana state line. Bronson was established quite early and had a Polish parish, St. Mary's, by 1867. This rural area still has an annual Polish festival to celebrate its ethnic heritage. Jackson, Michigan, had a large Polish population by 1920. This corresponded with the large influx of Poles early in the twentieth century. Jackson had several industrial concerns that employed many immigrants. By 1920 there were three parishes in Jackson: St. Joseph's, established in 1902, St. Stanislaus in 1920, and Holy Cross Polish National Catholic Church. The growth of the auto industry led to the movement of Poles to the Lansing area to work at Oldsmobile. Kalamazoo also had a large enough population to support a Polish parish, St. Mary's, by 1921.

The Grand Rapids area clearly had the largest Polish population in western Michigan. There were other settlements, however, in Hilliards, Belmont, Muskegon, Ludington, Manistee, and Free Soil. Many of these were farming communities.

The northwestern quadrant of Michigan had at least five Polish settlements. From 1889 to 1906 parishes were established in Cedar, Boyne Falls, Elmira, and Larks Lake. Most of these settlers in those parishes worked in the timber industry and/or farmed. The largest settlement was in Gaylord where St. Mary's Church eventually became the basilica for the Gaylord archdiocese. The 250 Polish families in Gaylord were mainly woodsmen and potato farmers.[17]

Readers from the metropolitan Detroit area may be surprised to discover that the Upper Peninsula of Michigan had significant Polish settlements. The first and ultimately the largest settlement was Calumet. Present day visitors to Michigan's Copper Country see small towns that look as though they have seen better days. During the copper boom it was one of the most populous areas in the state. Calumet, with about 90,000 residents, was the second largest city in Michigan and, some assert, it was almost named the state capitol. In 1872 there were only four Polish families and a few single men in Calumet. By 1875 there were enough Poles in Calumet to start the Calumet Polish Roman Catholic Stanislaus Kostka Benevolent Society to care for the sick, injured, and deceased member's families. The founders; John Zwirzchiowski, Anton Ozinski, Martin Fleus, Mace Mydowski and Valentine Nocozski, followed a Polish tradition of caring for the members of their families or communities. By 1882 a Polish church was built, St. Anthony of Padua, and by 1907 the parish had 1,259 members. Records from the Calumet and Hecla Mining Company indicate that "Austrians," the label assigned to Poles as well as Slovenians and Croatians, were second only to Finns as the largest foreign born group working in their mines.[18]

As mining expanded so did Polish immigration in the Upper Peninsula. Painsdale, south of Houghton, had many Poles working at the Champion Copper Mining Company. By 1894 five Polish residents: Michael Borskowski, Michael Joskobiak, Joseph Jonski, Joseph Glowzinski and Walter Kowalski organized the St. John Polish Miners' Society to care for the sick, injured, and deceased member's families. The Houghton County Directory of 1916 – 1917 listed eighty-five Polish families living in Painsdale. The area drew Poles even after the copper boom. Irene Wisniewski is a former displaced person who came to Painsdale with her husband in 1952 and raised a family. She was placed in a German concentration camp at age fourteen in 1940 and was liberated by American troops in 1945. She was even able to bring her mother to the United States from then communist Poland in 1972.[19]

The iron mining areas of the western Upper Peninsula were a popular draw for immigrant Poles. St. Michael's Parish in Ironwood was formed in 1891 by 250 Polish, Hungarian, Slovak, Slovene, Bohemian, and Croatian families. By 1920 the other nationalities formed another parish and St. Michael's was a Polish parish of 300 families.[20] Two other Polish settlements in Gogebic County were in Wakefield and Bessemer. Iron County had 764 Poles among 5,983 immigrants living in the county in 1910. The majority lived in Iron River where they had established Assumption Parish in 1903. Poles were fourth in population in the county behind the Finns, Italians, and Swedes.[21]

On the Lake Michigan shore of the Upper Peninsula there were several Polish settlements. Polish lumbermen first settled in Menominee and established St. Adalbert's parish in 1890. By 1906 there was a large Polish settlement eight miles east of Menominee called Sobieski, after the Polish king, John III (1674 – 96). The Poles in this area returned to their Polish agrarian roots and were mainly farmers. While the town no longer exists it was large enough at one time to have a Polish church, St. Mary's.[22]

Poles also settled in Bark River Township near the town of Spaulding. In 1911, six Polish families headed by Joseph Kosinski, Adam Yagodzinski, Antoni Skrobiak, Albert Kobacki, Felix Barr and Stanley Bass settled there. They were followed in 1914 by the families of Stanley Mroczkowski, Andrew Mroczkowski, John Kobos, George Grzyb and John Polkadowski. These groups were not unusual in that they migrated from the coalmines of Pennsylvania and Ohio and the cities of Pittsburgh, Cleveland, and Chicago. They had been farmers in the old country and took advantage of the opportunity to settle on land negotiated by the Polish National Alliance of America. In 1951 Pulaski Park (named after the American Revolutionary War hero) was built on US 2/US 41 on lakefront land donated by the Bark River Pulaski Club. In 1971 there were still fifty Polish American families in the township.[23]

Another Polish farming community existed at Goetzville in the eastern Upper Peninsula. This farming area was established earlier than the others mentioned, and the St. Stanislaus Kostka church, dedicated in 1897, is still an active parish. Altogether at least twenty-four Polish communities were established in the Upper Peninsula:

Hancock	Bessemer	Iron Mountain	L'Anse
Norway	Cedar River	Stephenson	Sault Ste. Marie
Ontonagon	Spalding	Fayette	Eagle Harbor
Atlantic Mine	Wakefield	Mass City	Vulcan
Laurium	Republic	DeTour	Houghton
Nadeau	Escanaba	Munising	Baraga

These clusters contributed greatly to making Poles the second largest ethnic group in the state of Michigan.[24]

Metropolitan Detroit

When John Gorecki arrived in Detroit in 1901 he followed a route taken by many others. He did not come to Detroit directly from Poland. Many Detroit Poles had first worked in textile mills in Massachusetts. Others had been recruited to work in the coal fields of Pennsylvania, southern Ohio, and Illinois. Still others had originally worked in steel mills in Pittsburgh and slaughterhouses in Chicago.

Eighteen-year-old John was an orphan in Poland. He was working as a laborer on a relative's farm when he heard that lumber companies needed single men to work in lumber camps in America. The trip was free and he only had to work for a year in the camps to pay for his pas-

Figure 3. John and Antoinette Gorecki's wedding picture, 1910. Courtesy of Dennis Badaczewski.

sage. It seemed like a good idea as he had no land or marketable skills in Poland.

While working in the lumber camp outside of Shingleton in Michigan's Upper Peninsula he heard others speak of the big city of Detroit. He had never lived in a city, but it could not be worse than the twelve hours a day, six days a week work he was doing in the camp, and there were many people in Detroit who spoke his language. One year to the day of his arrival in Shingleton, he left for the big city.[25]

Women did not travel alone a hundred years ago. Those who immigrated to America came either with their spouses, their families, or as children. The lone immigrants who went to the lumber camps, mines, and mills were male. Pioneer Polish women worked mainly in hotels and restaurants or as domestic servants. Their daughters might have worked in cigar factories, in stores as saleswomen and wrappers, in offices as clerks and typists, as teachers, or as sewing machine or punch press operators in factories.

In 1900 there were 285,704 people living in Detroit ranking it the thirteenth-largest city in America. The population had more than doubled in twenty years from 116,340 in 1880. This tremendous growth was not unusual in that Detroit's national ranking had only increased from seventeenth to thirteenth. Poles constituted about 17% of this total, or 48,570 people. The occupations of the 1,795 Polish women listed as employed outside the home by the Twelfth Census are as follows, listed by numerical importance:

1. tobacco and cigar factory operatives	6. teachers
2. servants and waitresses	7. packers and shippers
3. dressmakers	8. agricultural laborers
4. tailoresses	9. saleswomen
5. launderesses	10. clerks and copyists

These numbers do not include the self-employed.[26]

Like many other pioneering women, Polish women were mainly involved in homemaking. Napolska asserts that the most important factor contributing to the economic progress of Detroit Poles was the sense of thrift and the creative home management of the Polish woman. It was not unusual for these urban dwellers to have a large garden, a few chickens for eggs and meat, often a cow, a few pigs, ducks, and geese. At the same time either the cellar or backyard shed would have twenty to forty bushels of potatoes, a small barrel of salt, a large barrel of flour, a bushel of beans, and home-dried or canned fruits. In their "spare" time they would knit, sew, and embroider. It was a great deal of activity for the size of the average urban or suburban house.

Prior to 1900 Poles worked mainly laying railways, paving streets, digging sewers, and laying water pipes to develop the infrastructure of Detroit. Those who were able to find it preferred year-round work at American Car and Foundry, Michigan Central Depot, or various stove works, mostly as unskilled laborers. After 1900 the development of the auto industry attracted many skilled Polish workers. Many of these workers—mechanics, millwrights, diemakers, toolmakers, drafters and engineers, had their early training in Poland. Henry Ford, speaking of improvements in the auto industry, stated "The Polish workmen seem to be the cleverest of all the foreigners in making [cars]."[27]

Prior to World War I virtually all the Poles in Metropolitan areas of Detroit lived in the city. In 1914 over 100,000 Poles lived in the city of Detroit, comprising 24% of the total population. The majority lived in the east side neighborhood around Gratiot and St. Aubin or the west side neighborhood around Michigan and Junction.

By 1900 only 53% of the Poles were identified as laborers. The others either worked in skilled occupations in the auto industry, were professionals, or owned businesses. John Gorecki, for example, went to work for a Polish house painter in 1901 and later became a painting contractor, employing two or three crews of painters and plasterers recruited from more recent immigrants.

The immigrants usually built their own homes with the help of friends, relatives, and fellow parishioners. This do-it-yourself characteristic meant that a relatively small amount of money, between $400 and $600, would purchase land, a building permit, and materials. The reluctance of other groups to move to a predominately Polish neighborhood kept property values low. For comparison, immigrant German neighborhoods constructed homes for about $750 and native whites spent from $1,400 to $2,400. The Polish houses were typically of wood frame construction and were composed of three rooms in a line from front to back. Often the front room was rented out to another Polish family that was saving to build their own home. Nearly 70% of Polish families lived in multiple family dwellings, most containing two families. The typical Polish immigrant family consisted of a husband, wife, and three or four children, the highest number of any group in the city.[28]

The high rate of home ownership characteristic of Detroit's Poles suggests much about "Polishness" at the beginning of the twentieth century. Poland, as well as most European countries, practiced a system called primogeniture, the exclusive right of the eldest son to inherit his father's estate. Virtually all of a family's wealth was in the land it owned so primogeniture was a way to keep the family land in one piece. In old countries, the land could be quickly divided so that soon the land would be in very small parcels. An example: if someone had a section of land, 640 acres—a large parcel in Europe—and had four children, they would each inherit 160 acres. If the children each had four children, these grandchildren would have 40 acres of land. Under the same premise, great-grandchildren would inherit 10 acres and great-great grandchildren would inherit only 2.5 acres. In about 150 years a large estate would be reduced to many pieces of land the size of urban house lots. By giving all the land to the eldest son, primogeniture tried to ensure that a family's holdings would stay together.

In wealthy families the eldest son kept the land and the others went into the military or the priesthood. Daughters all hoped that their arranged marriage would be to an eldest son who owned his family's land. For wealthier Poles this problem was compounded by the varying nature of the borders. Those who lived in a part of Prussia, Austria, or Russia, were likely to have their land given to a loyal citizen of those countries. These Poles were anxious to have land in America that was bought and paid for.

Moreover, the vast majority of Polish immigrants were peasants. They owned no land at home in Poland, but worked and lived on another's property. Their families may have lived in the same house for generations, but it belonged to the eldest son of another family. If they were landowners, the oldest son usually stayed in Poland while younger males may have immigrated. For these people,, owning a house and land was their fondest dream. It was a dream deferred when they rented the front room of another family's home and saved money to build their own. Owning a house and the land it stood on was an American dream that had its roots in the class-system of the homeland.

Hamtramck

Hamtramck, a suburb of Detroit, is regarded as the quintessential Polish American city but it was not always so. Colonel Hamtramck, a Hungarian-born soldier under General Anthony Wayne, was the namesake for Hamtramck Township, organized in 1789 as one of the four original townships in Wayne County. The tiny city of Hamtramck, about one and one-half miles square, is all that remains of the township that once was bordered by the Detroit River on the south, and Lake Saint Clair on the east. The original Hamtramck settlers were Irish and German.

In 1910 the population of Hamtramck was 3,559. By 1920 it was the largest village in the country with 48,618 residents—the highest population increase for any urban place in the United States. It reached its peak population of 60,000 in 1928 and was the most densely populated city in the entire United States. In 1914 the Dodge Brothers Motor Car Company opened the Dodge Main Assembly Plant on Joseph Campau Avenue. Soon there were four auto factories within one-and-a-half miles of the intersection of Joseph Campau and Holbrook, all within walking distance of Hamtramck.[29] The employment opportunities that the auto industry provided encouraged the tremendous population growth in Hamtramck.

Hamtramck was a very comfortable place for Poles. For immigrants especially it was a place where one could remain Polish—speaking the same language, following the same religion, living by the same customs, as in Poland. As late as 1960, 52% of the Hamtramck population was of foreign stock, which the census defined as having a mother or father who was not born in the United States. According to the 1990 census, 44% of Hamtramck's residents identified themselves as Polish, and Poles comprised 73% of the foreign stock. As a youngster living in Hamtramck I regularly heard store clerks and customers conversing in

Polish. Our African American mailman spoke Polish with many of the people on his route. We even had one hour a day of Polish-language instruction at school.

The Great Depression of the 1930s led to near economic collapse in many places, especially in towns like Hamtramck that were totally dependent on the auto industry. Most autoworkers were laid off without the security net of unemployment insurance that is now common. Some of the unemployed moved to more rural areas for the meager existence available on small farms. Others drifted to areas of the country that had more employment possibilities. World War II, however, led to increased industrial activity as the auto industry quickly converted to manufacturing military hardware, and Detroit and Hamtramck boomed again.

Those returning from the war regained their jobs in the auto industry and many took advantage of the GI Bill to purchase new homes. America was becoming a more mobile culture with automobile ownership at its heart. A driveway and a garage came part and parcel in the pursuit of the American dream. The thirty-foot-wide lots common in Hamtramck and much of Detroit, however, did not allow for driveways. There was also a lack of empty land for new homes. Alleys created access to separate garages, newly-built behind the houses.

Increasingly people moved to the nearby suburbs. The newly expanded highway system allowed one to still work in urban auto plants while living in Roseville, Warren, or St. Clair Shores. Some people escaped the "foreign" stigma of Hamtramck and Detroit while others pursued the long-held Polish dream of land and a home. Soon, new auto plants arose on the more available land in the suburbs. Hamtramck became a place where grandparents lived and events like Paczki Day were celebrated; but, the population of Hamtramck and Detroit was growing increasingly older.

Besides having a lively club scene and artistic community, Hamtramck is still home to Polish bakeries, meat markets, churches, restaurants, and organizations. It is still a settling place for new immigrants from Poland, Eastern Europe, former Soviet states, and the Middle East. Like their predecessors many stay in Hamtramck until they have gained an economic foothold and are able to move to the outer suburbs.

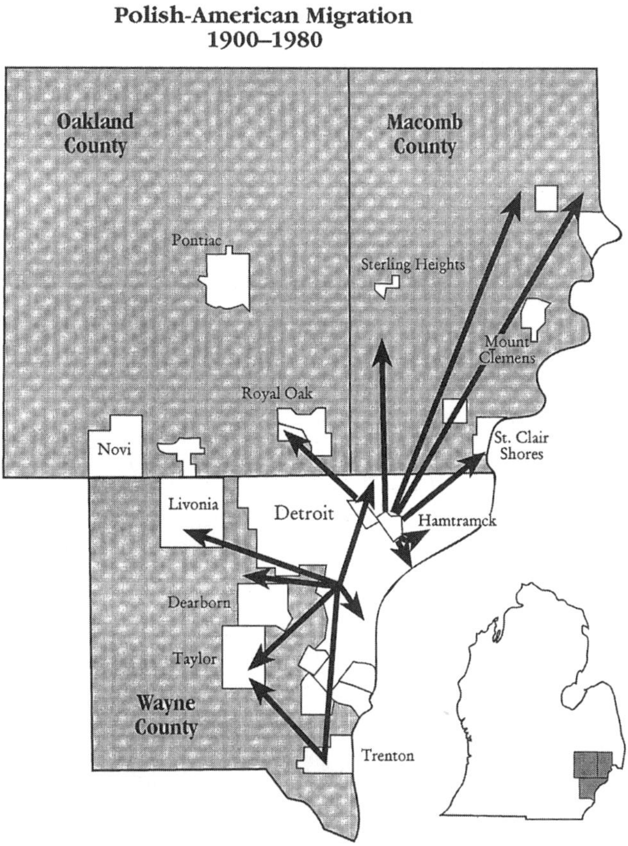

Polish-American Migration
1900–1980

Figure 4. Polish American Migration in Southeastern Michigan 1900–1980.

The city was cited recently as ranking sixth nationally for growth in average family size. According to the 2000 census Hamtramck has an average family size of 3.59 people, up from 3.05 in 1990. The national average is 3.14 people per family. The increased family size is due almost entirely to young immigrant families. Hundreds of immigrant families have arrived in the last decade accounting for the population growing by 25%. As in its former heyday, just 32% of Hamtramck school students are primarily English speakers. Students speak twenty-one other languages, from Arabic to Macedonian to Polish. Hamtramck's modest housing costs, tradition as an immigrant haven, and cosmopolitan culture have inspired its Polish born reputation as a welcoming place for new arrivals.[30]

During the summer and fall of 2000 the Hamtramck weekly newspaper, *The Citizen*, ran a thirteen-week series on the city's history, written by Walter Wasacz. His report provides a rich history of the political history of America's only city with an unbroken string of Polish mayors. Hamtramck became a city in 1922 with the election of Peter Jezewski as mayor. This roughly corresponded with the Volstead Act of 1919 that instituted the prohibition of the production and sale of alcoholic beverages in the United States.

In the early 1920s the Wayne County prosecutor called Hamtramck "the wild west of the middle west." The illegal gambling and drinking establishments that flourished were not owned by Poles, but local officials were compliant in letting them operate. Jezewski, the first mayor, was reelected in 1924 and sentenced to two years in the federal penitentiary in Leavenworth, Kansas, shortly thereafter. He ran for reelection in 1926 but was defeated by Stephen Majewski, a local attorney. Majewski exemplified the tension between maintaining Polish roots and trying to fit in with the larger society. He was born in Poland, came to America as a young boy, attended law school and then changed his last name to May to practice law. When he ran for mayor he changed his name back to Majewski to take advantage of his heritage.

In 1928, Dr. Rudoph Tenerowicz, a local physician and populist, was elected mayor. He was reelected in 1930, but in 1931 was indicted for vice crimes along with two city council members and the police chief. During the trial Tenerowicz appointed the aforementioned Jezewski to replace him and endorsed the ex-con for a third term in 1932. Joseph Lewandowski was elected in 1934 but was defeated by Tenerowicz in 1936 after he was pardoned by Governor William Comstock. Tenerowicz had served nine months of a three- to five-year sentence.

Reelected as mayor in the spring of 1938, Tenerowicz was elected to the U.S. House of Representatives in the fall of 1938. Poles in Hamtramck had learned well the power of the vote. In 1938, 17,000 of 25,000 registered voters (73%), voted. This was the largest percentage of any city in the United States, and was duplicated in the 1940 presidential election when Hamtramck was one of the largest two hundred cities in the nation.

Tenerowicz received 72,000 of 82,000 votes cast, an overwhelming Democratic majority. The power of the Democratic vote was exemplified when President Franklin D. Roosevelt came to Hamtramck to dedicate Keyworth Stadium, a Works Projects Administration (WPA) project. The legal problems of local politicians continued. Walter Kanar, a former state representative, was appointed mayor by the city council after Tenerowicz left for Washington. He was reelected in 1940 but resigned in 1942 before Governor Van Wagoner could remove him after Kanar was jailed for a month for giving evasive answers during questioning on charges of conspiring to give protection to gambling and prostitution establishments. Relative tranquility reigned in Hamtramck during the first of five terms of Dr. Steven Skrzycki (1942 – 1952) as mayor.

The Golden Age of Hamtramck probably occurred during the first mayoral reign of Albert J. Zak from 1952 to 1963. During this era Hamtramck was often regarded as the cleanest, safest, medium-size city in the country. Streets were swept weekly, trash was picked up from the alleys twice a week, and snow was cleared from all city streets and sidewalks by city employees. Hamtramck boasted one hundred police officers for a two-square-mile city. There was almost one city employee for every one hundred residents, with four hundred workers for a population of 43,000 people.

The major problem associated with this largess was that the city was losing population and therefore its tax base. In 1930 Hamtramck had 56,000 residents; by 1940, the population was 50,000 and by 1950 it was 43,000. Movement to the suburbs continued as the population fell to 34,000 in 1960 and 27,000 in 1970. When Zak resigned in 1963 to become Wayne County Commissioner, the city council president Joseph Grzecki became mayor. He was reelected in 1964, 1966, and 1968 by continuing the policies that made city services primary.

In 1970 Raymond Wojtowicz was elected mayor on an austerity platform that promised to balance the budget. Massive layoffs occurred among city employees, with the police department being reduced from 105 officers to 56 by 1973. Albert Zak defeated Wojtowicz in 1973 and returned as mayor. When Zak died of a heart attack in 1975, council president William Kozerski became mayor and was reelected in 1975 and 1977.

In 1979 Robert Kozaren was elected to the first of nine terms. An astute politician, he became the city's primary spokesperson establishing the Hamtramck Festival in 1980 during the Labor Day weekend, with the slogan "Hamtramck: A Touch of Europe in America." During his reign, Hamtramck was visited by Pope John Paul II, twice by President George Bush, and once by President Bill Clinton. The *Utne Reader* named Hamtramck as one of North America's fifteen hippest neighborhoods.

Hamtramck's changing population corresponded with America's. New immigrants from Yugoslavia, mainly Albanians and Macedonians, joined the Yemenis who had begun arriving in the late 1970s. In the 1990s, South Asians from Bangladesh and Pakistan began arriving. A trip to Hamtramck in 2001 reveals that the former home of the Alliance of Poles of America is now the B&H (Bosnia and Herzegovina) Bar and Grill. The Polish Roman Catholic Union hall is the Taj Mahal Indian restaurant, and the Polish Falcon's hall is the Motor Lounge, a popular nightclub. The 1990 census reported that Hamtramck is still 44% Polish, but the cultural mix is extremely rich.

By campaigning among these new ethnic groups, along with the growing artistic community, Gary Zych, a community college art instructor and sculptor defeated Kozaren in 1997 by three votes and was reelected as mayor in 1999.[31]

The 1990 census figures reveal that almost one out of every ten people living in Southeast Michigan is of Polish origin. The seven county region had 555,517 people of Polish ancestry with slightly more than 6% foreign born. Census figures base ancestry on self-identification and self-classification by people according to an ancestry group(s) with which they closely identify. Poland (3,109) follows only India (5,994), the Soviet Union (4,410), Canada (3,811), and Iraq (3,269) in the number of people who immigrated to Southeastern Michigan between 1990–1996.[32] Preliminary data from the 2000 census supplemental survey analysis indicates that 9,050,122 Americans said they are of Polish descent, out of a population total 273,643,269. This makes Poles the seventh largest ancestry group. Michigan's Polish population of 900,335 is third nationally behind New York (958,893) and Illinois (946,241), and represents 9.9% of the nation's Polish Americans.

The Jablonskis

George and Mary Jablonski are typical of the "DP" generation of Poles who came to Michigan after World War II. George, born in 1913, was a tailor when captured by the Russians during the Soviet invasion of Poland in September, 1939, and spent two years in a Russian prison. He then became a member of the Polish Home Army and the Polish Army 2nd Corps, serving as a sergeant in the cavalry in Iraq, Iran, Egypt, Italy, and England. Mary, born in 1922, was in a Nazi concentration camp in Udenberg, Germany. She was fortunately able to go to England rather than Russia after liberation because a family friend serving in the Polish division of the British army said that Mary was her sister. George went to England because of his service in the British army.

Figure 5. George and Mary Jablonski, courtesy of Gerry Gumul.

They met in 1946 and married in 1947 while George was working as a tailor in London. They arrived in Detroit on 24 April 1951 with their two-year-old daughter. George worked as a tailor in various men's clothing stores and Mary ran a dry cleaner and tailor shop attached to their house. They raised two children and have six grandchildren, including a grandson who attended the United States Air Force Academy. Retired, they live in Warren and are active in Polish veteran's groups, the American Polish Cultural Center in Troy, and the Alliance of Poles of America.[33]

The distribution of the current population indicates that Poles are predominantly in Wayne, Macomb, and Oakland counties.

Table 1. Geographic Distribution of the Polish Population

COUNTY	NUMBER OF POLES	PERCENTAGE OF COUNTY POPULATION
Wayne	220,025	8.9%
Macomb	154,187	15.4%
Oakland	119,945	8.2%
Livingston	13,303	8.1%
St. Clair	15,765	7.9%
Monroe	12,005	6.6%
Washtenaw	19,287	5.2%

The largest Polish communities are in Warren and Sterling Heights, both Macomb County cities. The Polish population differs little from the population as a whole regarding occupations. The following table lists the percentages for various occupational categories.

Table 2. Polish Occupations in Michigan

Managerial & Professional	29%
Technical, Sales, and Administrative Support	26%
Service	9%
Farming, Forestry, Fishing	1%
Precision Production, Craft, and Repair	20%
Operators, Fabricators, and Laborers	16%

The ties that the Polish population has to the auto industry are apparent in their occupational distribution. Twelve percent of the total workforce lists their occupation as precision production, craft and repair, as opposed to 20% of Polish workers.[34]

It is remarkable that a group of people who were classified by the American government as Russian, German, or Austrian when they arrived has managed to maintain an ethnic identity in their adopted country. The Poles seem to be bound together by their common Polish language, their Roman Catholicism, and their ethnic identity. This ethnic pride seems to have been enhanced by the challenges to Polish identity rather than diminished.

The new epicenter of Poles in Michigan appears to be in Troy, near Maple and Dequindre. As the Poles have left Hamtramck they are increasingly settling in the northwest area of Sterling Heights; 10% of Troy is of Polish ancestry. The Polish Plaza is a shopping center that caters to Poles with markets, a bookstore, a travel agency, a Polish bank, a restaurant, and a medical center. The Polish American Cultural Center and Our Lady of Czestochowa Catholic Church are across the street. Approximately 40,000 Polish Americans live within a five-mile radius of the plaza. Since their arrival in the 1800s, Poles continue to congregate in enclaves that promote and preserve their culture.[35]

Assimilation and Acculturation

Polish surnames were unfamiliar to both the eyes and ears of earlier settlers in Michigan. Polish immigrants who tired of mispronunciations and misspellings responded in a variety of ways. Some changed their names to English translations; Kowalski, the most common Polish surname, became Smith while Jaworowicz became Mapleton. Others were Anglicized; Walker for Walkowiak, Preston for Przekopowski, and Jarvis for Jaworski. Former Grand Rapids mayor Stanley Davis was originally Dyszkiewicz and former Grand Rapids judge Roman Snow had been Sniatecki. The majority, however, retained their "ski," "cki," and "wicz" endings and endured the problems.

Other name changes occurred for business and social reasons. John Covaleskie claims that his father and uncle disagreed on the spelling of their name when his father added an "e" to Covaleski. His uncle spelled it the Polish way, Kovaleski, and the third brother shortened his name to Coval. Jim Rapport claims his family name is Gwisdoniewicz but the government official at Ellis Island recorded "Rapport" because he could not spell Gwisdoniewicz and his sponsor, an uncle, was named Rapport. John Badaczewski told a story about applying for a loan to buy a business. He said that the deal was ready, but the banker asked him for references. He replied that his two brothers, Joe Badash and Frank Brady, would vouch for him. The loan was not approved.

Anna Mae Maday's study of Polish surnames in Saginaw used newspaper obituaries and personal interviews. She found that names were changed by shortening, translating into English, or retaining only the first letter. A few examples were:

Blazejewski-Blaze	Bocian-Stork	Brzeczkiewicz-Brink
Frydryszek-Frederick	Gwiazdowski-Starland	Jaroszewski-Jaro
Jaroszewski-Jaroh	Jaroszewski-Jaski	Maciejewski-Meyers
Milczewski-Miller	Morysiewicz-Morris	Nerring-Smith
Nienartowicz-Nye	Przysiewkowski-Miller	Schramkowski-Scham
Tarasiewicz-Tarras	Twarozynski-Twaro	Urbanowski-Urban
Wisniewski-Cherry	Wojciechowski-West	Zdzrynski-Smith

In spite of perceived pressures to the contrary many of these Smith's, Miller's and West's still identify themselves as Polish-Americans and retain their ethnic heritage.[36]

Acculturation means giving up the ethnic culture in favor of mainstream American culture, and certainly many Poles have done so whether or not they changed their names. Assimilation refers to the development of social and other relations with people outside of one's ethnic background. At least half of those who identify themselves as Poles have been assimilated by marriage. The fact that so many still identify with their ethnic heritage exemplifies strong cultural ties.

The Catholic Church

Poles, perhaps more than any other ethnic group, are closely identified with one religious group. While a few Poles are Protestant and some are Jewish, the vast majority of Poles are members of the Roman Catholic Church. For most it is a hallmark of their Polishness. In Europe, Poland was often administered by other countries. The Prussians and Austrians were usually Lutherans, the Russians were Eastern Orthodox. The Poles had two things that allowed them to remain Polish within moving borders—their religion and their language.

The Poles who immigrated to America and Michigan kept this allegiance. They chose to live in Polish neighborhoods, usually built around

Figure 6. Polish National Alliance, 1999. Courtesy of Suzan Mazer.

a Catholic Church staffed by Polish priests. Father Joseph Dabrowski established the first two Polish institutions of higher education in the United States. In 1882 he started a Felician Sisters seminary and normal school in Detroit. By 1900 the Felician sisters ran forty schools, about half of all the Polish parochial schools in the United States. His second notable achievement was Sts. Cyril and Methodius Seminary, opened in Detroit in 1886 to train Polish-speaking priests. The seminary moved to Orchard Lake in 1909 where it took over the site of the defunct Michigan Military Academy. The Felician Academy is now Madonna University in Livonia and Sts. Cyril and Methodius Seminary still exists in Orchard Lake along with St. Mary's Preparatory High School and St. Mary's College.[37]

These institutions were intended to preserve the Polish language and the Polish influence on Roman Catholicism. Mother Monica Sybilska, founder of the American Felician order, is reported to once have said to a young nun, "Sister, remember it was for the Polish language that I crossed the ocean."[38] At its peak there were ninety-four Polish parishes in Michigan, forty-one in metropolitan Detroit and fifty-three outstate. In the Detroit area the first Polish parish was St. Albertus, named after the first Polish saint Adalbert, dedicated in 1871. Currently there are thirty-two churches with predominantly Polish populations.

Table 3. Metropolitan Detroit Polish Roman Catholic Churches

Our Lady Queen of Angels	Assumption	Corpus Christi
Our Lady of Mt. Carmel	St. Albertus	St. Andrew
Our Lady Queen of Apostles	St. Bartholemew	St. Barbara
Our Lady Queen of Heaven	St. Cunegunda	St. Casimir
St. Francis de Assisi	St. Florian	St. Hedwig
Our Lady of Czestochowa	St. John Cantius	St. Helena
St. Stanislaus Kostka	St. Louis the King	St. Hyacinth
St. Thomas the Apostle	St. Josephat	St. Ladislaus
Sweetest Heart of Mary	St. Stanislaus	St. Stephen
Church of the Transfiguration	St. Steven	St. Lawrence[39]
Sts. Peter and Paul	St. Casimir (west side)	

These concentrations have had both positive and negative effects on Poles in Michigan.

Negatively, Poles have been prone to isolation in ethnic enclaves. While this has changed somewhat since the advent of suburban living, most early Polish immigrants actively chose to live near people who spoke and worshipped as they did. The Polish seminary at Orchard Lake is unique in America. Inevitably, the goals of the Polish clergy and Polish Catholics came into conflict with the church hierarchy. The Poles operated from a European model in which the church and the language were, for all intents and purposes, the country and the culture. The American church hierarchy's position was a mix of inclusion, centralization, and perhaps anti-Polish sentiment.

The Sts. Cyril and Methodius Seminary was operated exclusively to prepare Polish-speaking priests for Polish-speaking parishes. The American church hierarchy did not realize the depth of these convictions. During the time of Russian domination from 1945 until the 1990s and the success of the Solidarity movement, Poland was the only Soviet satellite that was allowed to keep its seminaries open. The Russians realized they could not maintain their control without this accommodation.

Problems with the church hierarchy in Michigan began soon after large groups of Poles arrived. The Poles resisted the trend toward American inclusion more forcefully than other ethnic groups. In Poland the church was the main source of resistance to foreign domination, while in America the Poles encountered a church leadership dedicated both to centralizing its authority and swift assimilation. St. Lawrence in Cheboygan was to be called St. Hedwig after the Polish saint, but Bishop Henry Richter of Grand Rapids refused to have a parish named after a Polish patron saint because he thought it would deter inclusion. Perhaps also it was because St. Adalbert's, formed in Grand Rapids in 1881, was now the basilica. St. Dominic in Metz (near Alpena) was not named St. Hyacinth for the same reason. The fact that Bishop Richter was from Prussia, one of the countries that had divided Poland, did not alleviate the situation.[40]

The best known of these controversies involved St. Albertus and its Polish immigrant pastor, Father Dominic Kolasinski. Kolasinski arrived in 1882 and quickly gained the widespread support of his parishioners. In 1885 the new church, financed by his parishioners, was the first church in Detroit to have steam heat and electric lights. Charges of sexual immorality and poor financial management against Father Kolasinski led the Prussian-born bishop of Detroit to transfer the flamboyant but controversial priest to the Dakota Territory. In December 1885, thousands of his working class parishioners rioted in an attempt to win his reinstatement. Following a Christmas Day march on the bishop's residence, three to five thousand of them gathered outside the store of John Lemke, a supporter of the bishop. A shot fired from the store killed one of the demonstrators. The next day outraged supporters of Kolasinski stoned the residence of another leading Polish merchant and Kolasinski opponent. A new bishop, John Samuel Foley, was consecrated in 1888 and allowed Kolasinski to return.

Although not formally reinstated, Kolasinski went ahead with plans to build an even grander church three blocks away from St. Albertus. The cornerstone of that church, Sweetest Heart of Mary, was dedicated in 1892 by a bishop of the Old Catholic Church. Despite a severe economic depression in 1893, the Gothic revival masterpiece was completed by the end of the year. The Vatican decided it could not ignore the large parish of 4,280 families, consisting of 19,000 people. In January, 1894 Bishop Foley was ordered to negotiate a reconciliation with Kolasinski. On February 18, the bishop accepted Kolasinski and his rebellious Polish parishioners back into the diocese.[41]

The conflict between Polish Catholics and the American Catholic Church was not exclusive to Michigan. In 1897 the Rev. Francis Hodur founded the Polish National Catholic Church (PNCC) in Scranton, Pennsylvania. His followers resented decisions made by the hierarchy in Rome and were determined to have a say in the selection of priests, conduct services in Polish, and teach the Polish language and culture. The PNCC became the only permanent major schism to fracture the Roman Catholic Church in America. While only about 5% of Polish Americans joined, it still has about thirty parishes and thirty thousand members.[42]

The first PNCC church in Michigan was Our Savior on Golgotha Church on the west side of Detroit, dedicated in 1916. Other PNCC churches in the Detroit area are All Saints and Sacred Heart of Jesus in Detroit, Holy Cross in Hamtramck, and Our Savior in Dearborn Heights. Two outstate churches are Our Saviors in Jackson, and Parafia Sw. Josefa in Standish.[43]

Perhaps the Polish struggle to retain some independence from the Roman Catholic Church in America has helped to reinforce their religious commitment. Poles are usually viewed as practicing Catholics. In 1968 Bishop Thomas Gumbleton of Detroit stated that 40% of the practicing Catholics in the Archdiocese of Detroit were Polish. In fact, Polish Americans represent 25% of the Catholics in the United States. According to the *Catholic Encyclopedia* no other group of American Catholics can boast of a greater percentage of churchgoing men than the Poles.

Poles in Michigan have also had high profile churchmen appointed from their ranks. Half of the Archbishops of Detroit, two of four, have come from the Polish clergy. Edmund C. Szoka was born and raised in Manistee and was appointed the first bishop of Gaylord. He then became archbishop of Detroit in 1981 and was named cardinal in 1988. He currently serves as the head of the Prefecture for the Economic Affairs of the Holy See at the Vatican in Rome, a division he is credited with modernizing. Adam Maida, who began his priestly vocation in Marquette, Michigan, became the fourth archbishop of Detroit in 1990.

Father Theodor G. Bateski

Father Theodor G. Bateski may have been the first American-born Polish priest in Michigan. He was born in Houghton on 9 November 1879, the son of Polish parents. He attended St. Mary's Seminary in Cincinnati and St. Francis Seminary in Milwaukee and was ordained in 1904 by Bishop Frederick Eis at St. Cecelia's Church in Hubbell. He went to Detour in the eastern Upper Peninsula in 1910 and served there until his retirement in 1960. He died in 1965.

Father Bateski built two churches, one burned, for the St. Stanislaus Kostka parish in Goetzville. Besides his spiritual achievements he took an interest in civic affairs serving three terms as president of the Detour Village Council and organized the first Chamber of Commerce in town. During the Depression of the 1930s he coordinated WPA projects in the eastern Upper Peninsula.[44]

Figure 7. Monsignor Bateski with his two spiritual and biological sisters. Courtesy of the U.P. Catholic.

Education

Thankfully the day of the Polish joke is over. For a period of twenty-five years, roughly 1965 – 1990, Polish jokes were the rage, all operating on the premise of the "dumb Polack." The basis of this phenomena is likely two-fold. The first might be regional. In the Upper Peninsula the same jokes were told in reference to Finnish-Americans, in Minnesota they were Swedish, and in the Southwest, Mexican. These groups had in common a large presence in the geographic region. The second commonality is identifying with their ethnic culture, often to the exclusion of others. Poles are known for their ties to their heritage and language. They often lived and worshiped with other Poles, and retained their home language to the exclusion of others. The stereotype of the "dumb Polack" arose in response to a mistrust and misunderstanding of these ethnic differences.

Outside of the United States, Poles have been viewed very differently. The University of Krakow dates from 1384, two years earlier than the first German university in Heidelburg. The University of Krakow was recognized internationally, as half of the students from 1433 – 1509 were foreigners. The University of Padua (Italy) arose in the Middle Ages as one of the premier European universities. From 1501 to 1605 more than one hundred students from Poland were enrolled annually and formed 25% of the student body. Mikolaj Kopernik (1473 – 1543) better known by his Latinate name, Copernicus, taught mathematics and astronomy at the University of Rome and is one of the most historically famous scientists. He was educated at the Universities of Krakow and Padua and was also a priest. His theory, now called the Copernican system, was the first modern heliocentric theory of planetary motion, positing the sun stationary at the center of the solar system with all of the planets revolving around it. This theory not only explained the seasonal cycles and the procession of the equinoxes but also made modern space travel possible.[45]

Poles have always been regarded as a literate people. For those who emigrated before 1900 the literacy rate was eleventh out of thirty immigrant nationalities. In fact, the contribution of Alexander Curtius (Kurcjusz) to the organization of education in America is indisputable.

In 1659 Peter Stuyvesant, governor of New Amsterdam, now New York, invited him to establish the second Latin school (the first being Harvard) in what is now the United States.[46] The last Polish king, Stanislaw Poniatowski, established the first public and later national library in Europe. In 1772 he established Europe's first official Ministry of Education. This literate tradition carried over to Michigan. The many schools established by the Felician and Franciscan Sisters produced a population that read from its earliest days. In 1887 Detroit Poles asked the Detroit Public Library to add Polish language books to its collection. By 1901 the number of Polish books owned by the library grew from 250 to 14,000. In 1898 the library reported that its Polish books circulated more than any others. By 1987, the Purdy Library of Wayne State University held over 200,000 books in Polish, on such diverse subjects as law, history, literature, and the sciences. As a child I remember my grandmother, Antionette Zielinski, who was born in the United States in 1891, reading two daily newspapers, the *Dzienek Polski* in Polish and the *Detroit Times* in English, even though she had only three years of formal schooling. She followed a long Polish tradition of literacy.[47]

Recipients of the Nobel Prize have included many Poles. The world's most famous woman scientist, Marie Sklodowska Curie, was born in Warsaw, Poland in 1867. She is one of only three individuals awarded two Nobel prizes in two categories. She won the Nobel for physics in 1903 in recognition of her research on the radiation phenomena and in 1911 for the advancement of chemistry by the discovery of the elements radium and polonium. Nobel prizes awarded to Poles are impressive both in their number and their breadth. In physics, prizes have been awarded to Albert Michelson (1907) of the University of Chicago, Maria Goeppert-Mayer (1963) of the University of California–San Diego, and Georges Charpak (1992), a Pole who settled in France after World War II. Besides Sklodowska-Curie, chemistry prizes were awarded to Walther Nernst (1920) who was born in Wabrzezno, Poland and worked at Berlin University and Roald Hoffman (1981) of Cornell University. Nobel prizes for Physiology or Medicine were awarded to Tadeus Reichstein (1950) of Basel University in Switzerland, Andrew Schally (1977) of the Veteran's Administration Hospital in New Orleans, and Gunter Blobel (1999) of Rockefeller University, New York.

Polish-born winners of Nobel prizes have been especially prolific in the field of literature. They have been awarded to Henryk Sienkiewicz (1905) author of *Quo Vadis*, Wladyslaw Stanislaw Reymont (1924) for his great national epic, *The Peasants*, Isaac Bashevis Singer (1978) of New York, who wrote impassioned narratives with roots in the Polish-Jewish cultural tradition, Czeslaw Milosz (1980) a Polish poet who taught at the University of California–Berkeley, Wislawa Szymborska (1996) Poland's foremost poetess, and Gunter Grass (1999) the Polish-born German writer. Poles have also been awarded three Nobel Peace Prizes; Lech Walesa (1983) the Solidarity trade union leader, Shimon Peres (1994) the Polish born foreign minister of Israel, and Joseph Rotblat (1995) a Polish-born British citizen for his efforts to diminish the role of nuclear arms in international politics. Clearly, the accomplishments of Poles have garnered international recognition.[48]

Closer to home Michigan Poles have distinguished themselves in the sciences. Felix Wladyslaw Pawlowski (1876–1951) immigrated to the United States in 1910 after designing, building, and flying his first airplane in France. Working as a mechanical engineer he contacted the major engineering schools in the country, proposing to offer courses in aeronautical engineering. However, most deans believed aeronautics would never amount to anything worthwhile. Fortunately Dean Cooley of the University of Michigan was a believer, and invited him to join the mechanical engineering department in 1912. He eventually became Guggenheim Professor of Aeronautics, spent the years 1915–17 designing and constructing airplanes for the War Department, built the wind tunnel at the University of Michigan, and conducted the first courses in Naval Aviation for the Naval Reserve Air Force.[49]

Emil Konopinski was born in Hamtramck and was president of the 1929 Hamtramck High School graduating class. He became a physicist and gained fame as the co-holder, with Edward Teller, of the patent for the hydrogen bomb. Dr. Teller claimed that Konopinski proved mathematically that the H-bomb would not ignite the atmosphere of the world or the ocean, allowing the bomb to be built. Dr. Konopinski retired from Indiana University and endowed, at the time of his death, the Joseph and Sophia Konopinski Memorial Physics Lectures to honor his parents.[50]

Steve Wozniak, who cofounded Apple Computer with Steve Jobs, has firmly established Michigan roots. His grandfather emigrated to Posen, one of Michigan's earliest Polish communities, where Steve's father was born and raised. Many Wozniak family members still reside in northeastern Michigan.

Michigan Poles differ very little from the total population in educational attainment. For southeastern Michigan the 1990 census reports the following:

Table 4. Polish Educational Attainment

No High School Diploma .23%

High School Diploma 28%

Some College 23%

Associate Degree 7%

Bachelor's Degree 12%

Graduate Degree 7%

Household income for 1990 reveals that over 33% of Michigan Polish families earn over $50,000.[51]

Data also indicate that Poles are well represented in all occupational categories. In the field of education fifty-eight individuals with Polish surnames are either superintendents or deputy superintendents of public school districts. While it is impossible to determine those who have had their surnames changed or who have married men with non-Polish names, this is a significant group in top leadership positions in Michigan's more than five hundred school districts. People like Leonard Rezmierski, Sandra Bozynski, Joseph Kukulski, Mary Cybulski, David Micinski, Sharina Dajnowicz, John Dardzinski, and Carolyn Wierda are ample evidence of Michigan Poles leading our schools.

Military

On 19 July 1980, President Jimmy Carter called Lt. Col. Matt Urban "The Greatest Soldier in American History" while presenting him with the Congressional Medal of Honor. *The Guinness Book of World Records* calls him the most decorated soldier in American history. His twenty-nine medals rank him above even Audie Murphy, who channeled his successful military career to Hollywood stardom. Urban's Medal of Honor citation referred to ten separate acts of bravery from 14 June to 3 September 1944 during the Normandy campaign. Early in the fighting in Northern France he was wounded twice while battling tanks with a bazooka. After shrapnel ripped into his leg, he was shipped back to England to an Army hospital, but within six weeks he had hitchhiked back to the front. Once there, he found his unit bogged down by German fire. He ran across the open ground to an unmanned American tank, and with machine gun bullets ricocheting around him, mounted the turret, climbed in and returned the enemy fire, routing the German position. He was nominated for the Medal of Honor by his commanding officer but the recommendation was lost before being re-discovered in the late 1970s. Urban never pursued the award himself. Born in Buffalo, New York, he came to Michigan after the war and served as recreation director of Port Huron for seven years, as director of the Monroe Community Center for sixteen years, and retired as director of the civic and recreation department of Holland, Michigan. His death in 1995 was a result of complications from a collapsed lung brought on by one of his seven war wounds.[52]

During World War I Polish Americans, many from Michigan, raised a division of 28,000 volunteer soldiers who fought alongside Polish forces in Europe. They were not being disloyal by volunteering to defend their historical home before the United States entered the war. When the United States entered the war 40,000 Polish names were on the roll of the first 100,000 to enlist, 40% of all early enlistees. More than 300,000 Polish immigrants and Americans of Polish descent served in World War I. While the Polish population of the United States was about 4%, Polish Americans accounted for 12% of the casualties of that war.[53]

In World War II the 900,000 Polish Americans who served in the Armed forces accounted for 17% of all enlisted men. Thirty thousand gave their lives. Hamtramck, Michigan, sent a larger percentage of its residents to the military than any other American city. These soldiers were fitting compatriots of the American Revolutionary War heroes Thaddeus Kosciusko and Casimir Pulaski.

Hamtramck also was the home of one of the most controversial soldiers of the Second World War. Private Eddie Slovik was the only

American soldier executed for desertion since 1864, during the Civil War. There were an estimated 20,000 deserters during the winter of 1943, many of whom fled to Paris. Most were given dishonorable discharges but General Dwight D. Eisenhower, Supreme Commander of the Allied Forces in Europe and a future president of the United States, felt an example had to be made. Slovik was tried and convicted by a military court on 11 November 1944 and executed by a military firing squad. The details of the case remain controversial. Slovik had stated he would serve but would not go into combat because he was afraid he would do something to put his comrades at risk. The case led to a book written in 1954 and a 1974 television movie starring Martin Sheen, who also played the President of the United States in the television series, *The West Wing*. Among those working for a posthumous pardon for Slovik are Bernard Calka, former Macomb County Commissioner and past commander of a VFW post in Sterling Heights, and Stephen Osinski, a retired judge. They are supported by former Capt. Benedict Kimmelman, a member of the nine-man court martial board that condemned Eddie and wrote "His execution was a historic injustice."[54]

Politics

Poles in the United States faced a dilemma. They had never lived in a democracy and had never had the opportunity to vote. They came from Austria, Russia, or Prussia in situations where they were marginalized as residents in what they viewed as a foreign country. Not having a political home, they concentrated on preserving their Polishness through language, religion, culture, and tradition. At the same time they were fiercely democratic and had a long history of seeking the vote. The previously mentioned first labor strike in America was about political freedom, as were the heroics of Revolutionary War patriots Pulaski and Kosciuzko. Poles in Michigan applied these characteristics to their role in the American political system.

The first elected Pole in Michigan was Lawrence Kowalski, who served as a member of the County Board of Supervisors representing Presque Isle Township in 1871. Lawrence Przybyla joined the board in

1873. Both of these men represented the Poles who settled in Posen. Felix A. Lemke was the first Polish elected official in Detroit. He served as Justice of the Peace for forty-seven years beginning in 1876. He presided over more than 100,000 cases, a record in its time unsurpassed by any judge in the United States.[55]

Only two Poles served as state legislators in the nineteenth century: Adolph Jasnowski in the 1880s and Charles Petrowsky in the 1890s. The first statewide official was Lucian Koterski, elected Secretary of State in 1904. The early paucity of Polish politicians was related to two factors. First, the largest wave of Polish immigrants was yet to come. Secondly, many of the immigrants were illiterate and most lived in Polish communities where they did not have to learn English. As Poles learned English and became U.S. citizens, their political power increased.

As Poles became citizens they also became a political force. Although they are often thought of as overwhelmingly Democratic, the first Pole elected to the U.S. Congress was the first Republican Polish congressman in the United States, John B. Sosnowski of Detroit elected in 1924. Michigan was a Republican state at the time. Sosnowski also chaired the Wayne County Board of Supervisors in 1920 and ran for mayor of Detroit in both 1931 and 1933. He had served as Federal Appeal Agent of the U.S. Selective Service—the draft board—during World War I. Among other firsts, John Kronk was the first Pole elected to the Detroit Common Council in 1919 and Stanley Bahorski was the first Polish state senator, serving from 1923 - 26.[56]

The Polish commitment to the Democratic Party truly began with the landslide election of Franklin D. Roosevelt as President of the United States in 1932. The Depression had a devastating effect on Polish Americans with rampant unemployment, coupled with few social services, leading to economic problems they had not seen since leaving Poland. The Roosevelt landslide led to Democrats George Sadowski, John Dingell (Dziegielewski), and John Lesinski being elected to Congress from the 1st, 15th, and 16th congressional districts. In the same election, seven of Detroit's seventeen state representatives were Polish. Baginski, Brelawski, Dombrowski, Jurkiewicz, Kaminski, and Romanski were joined by Joseph C. Roosevelt who had changed his name to a more familiar political one.[57]

The 1st Congressional District was the most Democratic, in terms of party registration, in the country. As a youngster I recall the annual Labor Day parade in Hamtramck, which was always attended by the governor and often by the President of the United States. I recall as a child seeing President Truman; likewise I saw President George Bush with my children in 1992. They both gave an obligatory greeting in Polish. After re-districting, the 14th Congressional District—including northeast Detroit, Hamtramck, Warren, and Sterling Heights—was the third most Polish in the country with 22% of the residents claiming Polish ancestry. A district in south Milwaukee, Wisconsin is first with 26%. In 2001 there are three members of Congress, all Democrats, with Polish surnames; Jim Barcia of the 5th district in Bay City, Bart Stupak of the 1st district in the Upper Peninsula and northern Michigan, and John Dingell Jr. of the 16th district in western Wayne and Monroe counties.

The Dingell and Lesinski political families deserve further discussion. John Dingell was a New Deal Democrat who remained true to his ideals and served from 1932 to 1955, when he died suddenly. His son, John Dingell Jr., ran in a special election and easily won. Still in office as of 2001, Dingell Jr. is one of the most powerful members of Congress. He is a strong supporter of national health care, as was his father, and has chaired the House Energy and Commerce Committee. Regarded as a fierce fighter both for his constituents and his principles, he was referred to as "kind and gentle" in a 1990 House speech. William Clay, a congressman from Missouri and friend of Dingell, jokingly said, "calling John Dingell kind and gentle is like calling a termite an interior decorator." The "little Polish lawyer from Detroit" had made his mark.[58]

Having grown up above his family's grocery store in Hamtramck, John Lesinski, like Dingell, was elected to Congress in the Roosevelt landslide of 1932. Also like Dingell, he died in office in 1950 and was succeeded by his son, T. John Lesinski. T. John served in Congress until 1964 when he ran for lieutenant governor of Michigan. Leo Nowicki, elected in 1944, was the only other Polish lieutenant governor of the state. At that time the candidates for governor and lieutenant governor were not elected as a team. The unlikely happened in 1964 when the popular Lesinski, a Democrat, was elected lieutenant governor while George Romney, a Republican and president of American Motors, was elected

Frank and Lillian Szymanski

Frank Szymanski might define the term scholar-athlete. He studied physics at Notre Dame, taught physics at the University of San Francisco, and worked on the Manhattan Project developing the atom bomb. He also served as Michigan's elected Auditor General and went on to serve as a Probate Judge in Wayne County for twenty-eight years.

Athletically, Frank was selected to the All-Time All State football team by a Detroit sports reporter for his play at Detroit's Northeastern High School. He was also captain of the football team at Notre Dame in 1943. A story

Figure 8. Frank Szymanski while at Notre Dame, courtesy of David J. Szymanski.

about Frank appeared in the popular book, *Chicken Soup for the Soul*. While at Notre Dame he was called to testify in a civil action. Notre Dame football coach Frank Leahy had come to court to make sure his star center was not just skipping classes.

"Are you on the Notre Dame football team," the judge asked.

"Yes, sir," came the reply.

"How good are you?" was the next question.

Szymanski seemed uneasy as he answered, "Sir, I'm the best center to ever play at Notre Dame."

Coach Leahy was surprised at the answer coming from the modest, unassuming athlete and asked why he had answered that way.

Szymanski's response was, "I had to do it coach. I was under oath."

Drafted in the first round by the Detroit Lions, he went on to play professional football with the Lions, Green Bay Packers, Philadelphia Eagles and Chicago Bears. In addition to his legal duties, Szymanski also founded the Detroit Crisis Club, a charitable organization that helped people in need; he also helped found the NFL Alumni Association.

Born and raised on Detroit's eastside, Lillian Mikula Szymanski attended Northeastern High School where she later taught English. She graduated from the University of Michigan and married fellow Northeastern graduate and Probate Judge Frank S. Szymanski.

Together they founded Kielbasa College, an informal learning environment where students learned the art of making Polish sausage while enjoying an afternoon in the Szymanski home in Grosse Pointe Park. "Diplomas" were awarded to successful students after the festivities, which hosted hundreds annually for more than fifteen years.

Lil was proud of her Polish roots and after raising seven children, four of whom became attorneys and one a Probate judge, she became the editor of the Polish Weekly newspaper also known as the *Tygodnik Polski.* The day she died, 26 July 2000, she was preparing for a meeting of the Board of Directors of the paper and going to dinner with son Michael who has assumed the duties of editorship.[59]

Figure 9. *Lillian Szymanski, courtesy of David J. Szymanski. Photograph by Mary Ann Maisano.*

governor. Romney reportedly stated that he was afraid to leave the state because of what the acting governor might sign. In any case, the law was changed, and 1964 was the last election in which the governor and lieutenant governor could be of different parties.

In his later years T. John became a prominent jurist. He was a judge on the first State Appeals Court and served as chief justice. After retirement he was appointed by the State Supreme Court in the early 1980s to manage the Detroit Recorder's Court because of the huge backlog in cases.

Polish Michiganians have been especially prominent in the legal field. The Polish Bar Association, called the Advokats, continues to be a prominent group. Many Polish judges have served and are serving at the local, state, and national levels. Arthur A. Koscinski was the first

Polish American federal district court judge in Michigan appointed in 1945. Thaddeus Machrowicz was a U.S. Congressman from Hamtramck who served from 1950 until he was appointed a federal district judge in Cincinnati in 1961. He was succeeded in Congress by another Pole, Lucien Nedzi.

Roman Gribbs (Gryzb) was an assistant Wayne County prosecutor from 1956 to 1970, when he was elected mayor of Detroit. He served one term, 1970–73. Following the movement of Poles to the suburbs, Carl Marlinga is the longtime prosecuting attorney for Macomb County and a frequently mentioned Democratic candidate for statewide office.

Frank Schemanske was the longest serving judge on Detroit's Recorders Court. Frank Szymanski (same pronunciation, different spelling) was a Wayne County Probate Court judge for twenty-eight years.

Michigan Poles are well represented in the state legislature. Following national trends, they are no longer exclusively Democratic, but representative of both parties. David Jaye (Jodlowski) a Republican from Clinton Township is the only identifiably Polish state senator. As of the 2000 election Republican office holders in the House are Ron Jelinek (78th district), Mike Kowall (44th district), Andrew Raczkowski (37th district), and Gary Woronchak (15th district). On the Democratic side Steve Pestka (76th district), Michael Switalski (27th district), and Paul Wojno (28th district) are legislators with Polish surnames. There are most probably other Poles with unidentifiable names due to marriage or family name changes. Currently, the prosecutors of two of Michigan's three largest counties are Polish Americans: David Gorcyca of Oakland County and Carl Marlinga of Macomb County.

Sports

Polish Americans are perhaps best known by non-Poles for their achievements in various athletic endeavors. The Fighting Irish of Notre Dame have had so many Polish players that Knute Rockne, their most famous coach, said he picked his players by their last names. "It's a cinch," he said, "When I can't pronounce 'em, they're good."[60] Michigan Poles have more than upheld this tradition.

During the 1950s and 1960s St. Ladislaus High School in Hamtramck was a perennial baseball champion winning Catholic League and City Championships. Among their stars were Steve Gromek, a longtime pitcher for the Cleveland Indians, Ted Kazanski, the first six figure "bonus baby" who received a $100,000 signing bonus from the Philadelphia Phillies and played shortstop for them, and John Paciorek who signed a large bonus with the Houston Colt .45's (now the Houston Astros) in 1961.

John Paciorek was the first of three brothers to play Major League baseball, tying a record achieved by the Dimaggios and Alous. Tom Paciorek graduated from Orchard Lake St. Mary's High School and played for almost twenty years with the Los Angeles Dodgers, Chicago White Sox, Atlanta Braves, Seattle Mariners, New York Mets, and Texas Rangers. He currently is a television analyst for the White Sox, WGN television, and Fox Sports Net. The youngest brother, Jim, also graduated from St. Mary's and earned All-State honors in three sports. He later was an All-American at the University of Michigan and played professionally for the Milwaukee Brewers.

Hamtramck High School was known for its outstanding tennis teams and holds the record for state tennis championships. It was especially noted for its women's tennis teams featuring future professionals such as "Peaches" and "Plums" Bartkowicz, Fran Gruda, and Phylis Saganski Laurala, current boy's and girl's coach at Iron Mountain High School. Jane ("Peaches") Bartkowicz was ranked as the fourth-best woman tennis player in the United States in the mid-1960s and is generally regarded as the best female tennis player ever to come out of the Detroit area. Hamtramck's Fred Kovaleski won the national amateur singes tennis title in 1947.

While the Detroit Lions have almost always had at least one Polish player, currently including Scott Kowalkowski and Pete Chryplewicz, both of whom grew up in Michigan, few have had the tenure of the Kowalkowski family. Bob Kowalkowski played for the Lions from 1966 to 1976 and Scott has been with them since 1994. Judy Kowalkowski, Scott's mother, is also the Lions' manager of accounting operations.[61]

Michigan Poles have also excelled in Olympic sports. Janet Lynn was a world-renowned figure skater and Tara Lipinski of West

Stanley Ketchel

Stanley Ketchel (Stanislaus Kiecal) was born in Grand Rapids of Polish immigrant parents on September 14, 1887 and baptized at St. Adalbert's Church. He

left farm life at 15 and "rode the rails" in the American West where he fought his way from the hobo jungles to a professional boxing career. Ketchel was dubbed the "Michigan Assassin" for his ferocious boxing style and won the world middleweight boxing championship on February 22, 1908.

He is generally regarded as the best middleweight boxer ever. His most famous bout was for the heavyweight championship of the world against Jack Johnson of The Great

Figure 10. Stanley Ketchel ca. 1908, World Middleweight Champion. GRPL Mich. Rm. Copy photo coll. (185). Courtesy of the Michigan and Family History Department, Grand Rapids Public Library.

Bloomfield was the 1998 Winter Olympic gold medal winner. Tara, the United States and world champion at age fourteen and Olympic champion at age fifteen, replaced the legendary Norwegian Sonja Henie as the youngest woman ever to be crowned the world's best skater.

In 1973 The National Polish American Sports Hall of Fame was established in Detroit. It began as the idea of four men; Leon Zarski, an elementary school teacher who organized Polish American Night at Tiger Stadium, Ed Browalski, a sports writer and official scorekeeper for

White Hope fame. Ketchel, weighing 158 pounds versus Johnson's 210, almost knocked the seemingly invincible champion out before being defeated. Sadly, on 15 October 1910 Stanley was shot and killed by a jealous farmhand while training in Montana. Stanley Ketchel was 23.[62]

Figure 11. Stanley Ketchel's funeral, 20 October 1910. Grand Rapids Public Library Photo Collection (54). Courtesy of the Michigan and Family History Department, Grand Rapids Public Library.

the Detroit Tigers, John Kiemba, president of the Polish American Chamber of Commerce, and Fr. Ted Blaszczyk, pastor of Our Lady Queen of Apostles Church in Hamtramck. In 1982 the NPASHF museum was established at the Orchard Lake St. Mary's campus, making Michigan the permanent home of this national hall of fame.

The requirements for induction include that nominees be at least half Polish. All amateur athletes are eligible; collegiate athletes not continuing into the professional ranks are eligible two years after their collegiate participation ends; professional athletes are eligible two years after retirement from the sport. As of June 2001 there have been eighty-three inductees. Fourteen of the athletes have Michigan ties. Lou Creekmur an All Pro with the Detroit Lions; Forest Evashevski, an All-American at the University of Michigan and later head coach at the University of Iowa; Leon Hart, an All American at Notre Dame and All-Pro with the Detroit Lions; and Frank Szymanski of Notre Dame and the Lions, all represent football. Steve Gromek, Tom Paciorek, Frank Tanana (born and raised in Detroit and a member of the California Angels and Detroit Tigers), and Alan Trammell of the Detroit Tigers represent baseball. Other Michigan Hall members are bowler Billy Golembiewski, boxer Stanley Ketchel, figure skater Janet Lynn, world champion weightlifter Norbert Schemansky, Detroit Piston basketball player Kelly Tripucka, and professional golfer Al Watrous.[63]

The fact that an organization like the National Polish-American Sports Hall of Fame exists and was begun in the late twentieth century and early twenty-first century says much about the Polish experience in Michigan and America. No other ethnic group that has been in this country for four generations or longer is still so associated with their heritage. The largest ethnic group in Michigan by self-identification is the Germans but there are few German clubs, restaurants, social and civic organizations, or sports halls of fame remaining. The same can be said for most other white ethnic groups.

These differences exist because, first, the Poles have spent much of their history trying to be Poles. The immigrants who came 100 or 125 years ago were Polish by language, religion, and culture, but not as members of a particular nation-state. America allowed them to retain rather than submerge their heritage. The ability to have Polish churches, Polish social clubs; Dom Polskis, Polish Falcons, Polish National Alliances, and Polish business and civic groups had been a forbidden activity in Europe.

Second, Poles have been immigrating over a long period of time. The earliest Poles assimilated quite easily. The second and largest group, which arrived between 1880 and 1920, held on to their collective ethnic identity for years but are now assimilated. The third group arrived after World War II and their second and third generations are also now assimilating. A fourth group came after the disruptions in Poland in the 1980s. A fifth group, the quota immigrants, are arriving now. Currently, Poland holds a lottery among eligible potential immigrants because the numbers of people desiring to enter the United States exceeds U.S. quota restrictions. These waves of immigrants have done much to keep Polonia alive.

Finally, parts of Polish culture have been incorporated into mainstream Michigan. Polish restaurants draw customers from the mainstream. Polish food products are available in mainstream markets and non-Poles prepare Polish recipes. (see recipes included in text). Paczki Day is a growing phenomenon. The Polish equivalent of Fat Tuesday, the day before Ash Wednesday, began in Polish bakeries throughout the Detroit area. Recently, mainstream supermarkets sell paczki, a jelly-filled deep fried, sugar glazed donut, the week of Ash Wednesday. Since 1997 Paczki Day has even spread to the Upper Peninsula. Poles and non-Poles also attend a variety of Polish festivals, parades, and "days" throughout the state.

Figure 12. Pazcki Day in Hamtramck, courtesy of The Citizen *(Hamtramck, Mich.).*

Polish Recipes

If you aren't Polish you might want to be after trying these recipes. A lifetime of eating Polish food leads me to believe these are the best examples of three popular Polish dishes. Enjoy!

Czarnina (Duck Soup)

1 duck, cut up
½ cup duck's blood (ask your butcher—they can find it dried)
1 box prunes and any other dried fruit: apples, pears, raisins
    (optional other than prunes)
1 bay leaf
salt to taste

Place the rinsed duck in soup pot, add enough water to cover and more. Bring to a boil. Skim off the scum as it forms. Add the bay leaf, prunes, and any other fruit, and salt to taste. Bring to a boil and keep simmering until the duck and fruit are soft.

Put the blood in a bowl and add 1 tablespoon flour and mix till smooth. Then add a little of the broth and mix well. Combine the blood, flour, and broth in this way until you have a 2 cups of broth in the blood mix. Add all the blood mix to the soup, mix well and let come to a boil. Best served with potato dumplings but can use noodles.

—*Helen Pucko Warren, Michigan*

Golabki (Stuffed Cabbage)

One 2- to 3-lb. head of cabbage (make sure leaves are loose)
1 lb. ground beef (or venison)
1 lb. ground pork
1 medium onion chopped
½ stick butter or margarine
1 cup cooked white rice
1 egg
Three 10¾-oz. cans tomato soup
4 cans of liquid reserved from boiling cabbage
1 small can (14 oz.) sauerkraut
salt and pepper to taste

Preheat oven to 450°.

Cut the core from the cabbage, wash and put in large pot of boiling water. The water should almost cover the head of cabbage. Cook until the leaves soften, turning the cabbage as it cooks. Leaves should be slightly soft. They will fall off the head as they soften. Remove them and drain on paper towels. Save liquid from the pot.

While the cabbage is cooking sauté the chopped onions in the butter or margarine until softened. Do not brown. Let cool.

Mix meat onions, cooked rice and egg. This is a bland dish so liberally season with salt and pepper.

Take each whole leaf and cut off the hard part of the main vein on the back of the leaf. This will help when rolling them. If leaves are very large they can be cut in two.

Place 2 or 3 Tbs. (depending in leaf size) of meat mixture in bottom of leaf and roll up, folding in leaf as you are rolling.

After you can no longer use the leaves chop the remaining cabbage and mix with the drained sauerkraut in the bottom of the pan—12" by

16" and 2½" deep. Place the cabbage rolls on top of the mixture in single layer 3 across. Take reserved cabbage water and mix with the tomato soup. Pour the soup mixture over the cabbage rolls to just cover the rolls in liquid. Cover the pan with foil. Place the pan in a 450° oven and cook for 30 minutes. Turn oven down to 400° and cook covered for another 30 minutes.

Tips: Let the cabbage rolls rest before serving. It's best to cook them the day before. Warm them, covered, in a 400° oven until they start bubbling. You can add more liquid if necessary. They go well with mashed potatoes, using the liquid as gravy. Leftovers freeze well and can be microwaved.

—Mary Wojcik Marquette, Michigan

Cruszciki (Angel Wings)

1 cup sour cream
4 egg yolks
2 cups sifted flour
1 tablespoon brandy (optional)
1 or 2 cups powdered sugar
Shortening for deep frying

Add all or enough flour to egg yolks, brandy, and sour cream to make a soft dough, kneading until smooth. Roll out very thin, ⅛ inch, cut into diamond shapes. Make a slit in center, pull one end through slit, deep fry until very light brown. Drain on paper towel. Dust with powdered sugar when cool.

—Lottie Gadzinski, St. Clair Shores, Michigan

Nobody said this meal would be Heart Smart! Enjoy!

Notes

1. Albert Q. Maisel, "The Poles Among Us," *Reader's Digest*, June 1955, 2; see also Joseph A. Wytrwal, *Behold! The Polish Americans* (Detroit: Endurance Press, 1977), 534.

2. *Poles in Michigan*, pamphlet from Hamtramck Public Library (Detroit: Associated Poles in Michigan, 1953), 22.

3. Joseph A. Wytrwal, *The Polish Experience in Detroit*, (Detroit, Endurance Press, 1992).

4. Leonard S. Chrobot, "Poles," in *Ethnic Groups in Michigan*, ed. James M. Anderson and Iva A. Smith (Lansing, Michigan Council for the Arts, 1983), 28.

5. Allan R. Treppa, "Parisville: Michigan's First Polonia," in *A Wind Gone Down: West-Running Brook* (Lansing, Michigan History Division, Michigan Department of State, 1978), 47–50.

6. Chrobot, "Poles," 219.

7. Wytrwal, *Behold! The Polish Americans*, 22; see also Chrobot, "Poles," 219.

8. Wytrwal, *Behold! The Polish Americans*, 553.

9. Ibid., 34.

10. Helen Znaniecka Lopata, *Polish Americans*, 2d ed. (New Brunswick: Transaction Publishers, 1994), 8.

11. Ibid., 9.

12. Lopata, *Polish Americans*, 215.

13. Edward A. Skendzel, "Polonian Settlements in Michigan," *The Eaglet 3*, no. 1, (January 1983): 2–15. *The Eaglet* is a publication of the Polish Genealogical Society of Michigan.

14. The interview with Mr. Wend was conducted by M. Russell Magnaghi, a historian at Northern Michigan University. The interview was done on 21 May 1984 and transcribed by Dr. Magnaghi on 11 May 2001.

15. Skendzel, "Polonian Settlements in Michigan," 9.

16. Peter Slavcheff began the original work on the Poles in Michigan project. His untimely death in 1994 left it unfinished. Reading his unpublished work has been extremely helpful.

17. Skendzel, "Polonian Settlements in Michigan," 2–15.

18. Arthur W. Thurner, *Strangers and Sojourners: A History of Michigan's Keweenaw Peninsula* (Detroit: Wayne State University Press, 1988), 147, 148, 349.

19. Marcia Goodrich, "Polish Woman Was Slave for Third Reich," *U.P. Catholic*, 19 January 2001, 1, 4.

20. "St. Michael's became 'Polish,'" *U.P. Catholic*, 24 January 1986, 4.

21. Ted Bays, Florence Brumm, and Russell Magnaghi, *Immigrants in Iron County, Michigan: 1910 Federal Census* (Marquette: Belle Fountaine Press, 1986) 13.

22. Skendzel, "Polonian Settlements in Michigan," 2–15.

23. "Bark River Centennial 1871–1971" (booklet, 1971), 105, 119.

24. Skendzel, "Polonian Settlements in Michigan," 9

25. Interview with Geraldine Kemichick, 30 January 2001, about her maternal grandfather John Gorecki.

26. Mary Remigia Napolska, O.S.F., *The Polish Immigrant in Detroit to 1914*, vol. 10 of *Annals of the Polish Roman Catholic Union Archives and Museum* (Chicago, 1946), 29–37.

27. Ibid.

28. Slavcheff, "Poles in Michigan," ms.

29. Frank Poma, Dennis Grzych, and Laurie Singer, "Hamtramck: Population Change 1930–1970," ms., [September 1972], Albert J. Zak Memorial Library, Hamtramck, Michigan, 7, 20.

30. Gordon Trowbridge and Christopher M. Singer, "Metro Area Draws Immigrants," *Detroit News*, 27 May 2001, sec. C-2, 3. sec. C-2, p. 3.

31. Walter Wasacz, *The Citizen*. Mr. Wasacz's thirteen-part series was crucial in gathering this information on Hamtramck. The following are the stories, along with their dates: "Wild West of the Middle West," 13 July 2000; "Power, Corruption, Vice," 20 July 2000; "1930s: When Scandal Ruled," 27 July 2000; "Slugging It Out in the 1940s," 3 August 2000; "Living Large in the 1950s," 10 August 2000; "Era of Big Spending Crashes," 17 August 2000; "1970s: A Decade of Crisis," 24 August 200; "A Star is Born," 31 August 2000; "A Decade of Dreams and Debts," 7 September 2000; "A Tower of Power," 14 September 2000; "A New Decade, New Faces," 21 September 2000; "The Times, They Were a-Changin,'" 21 September 2000; and "New Generation Takes Reins Over Divided City," 5 October 2000.

32. "Patterns of Diversity and Change in Southeast Michigan," Community Foundation for Southeastern Michigan website: *www.comnet.org/local/ orgs/comfound/respub/diversit/pat5*, Section V: Ancestry and Ethnic Origin.

33. The author conducted an interview with Mr. And Mrs. Jablonski on 5 October 2000.

34. Ibid.

35. Marsha Low, "Old World, New Home," *Detroit Free Press*, 7 July 2001, A, 3.

36. Anna Mae Maday, "Saginaw County Poles," *The Eaglet 3*, no. 1 (January 1983): 90.

37. "Poles in Michigan," 34–59

38. Wytrwal, *The Polish Experience in Detroit*, 142.

39. James M. Anderson, *Ethnic Organizations in Michigan* (Detroit, Ethnos Press, 1983), 97–98.

40. Skendzel, "Polonian Communities in Michigan," 2–15.

41. Slavcheff, "Poles in Michigan," 71–74.

42. Lopata, Polish Americans, 61; see also Thomas Okasinski, "Polish National Catholics," in *Michigan Challenge*, Michigan State Chamber of Commerce, April 1972, 29.

43. Anderson, *Ethnic Organizations in Michigan*, 98.

44. *Our Sunday Visitor*, 12 September 1965, 2.

45. Wytrwal, *The Polish Experience in Detroit*, 201.

46. Bogdan Grzelonski, *Poles in the United States of America 1776–1865* (Warsaw: Interpress, 1976), 11.

47. Slavcheff, "Poles in Michigan"; and Wytrwal, *Behold! The Polish Americans*, 22.

48. Nobel Foundation's website *http://main.amu.edu.pl/~zbzw/ph/sci/nobel. htm.*

49. University of Michigan website: *www.engin.umich.edu/dept/aero.*

50. Wytrwal, *The Polish Experience in Detroit,* 299; see also *www.physics. indiana.edu/konopinski.*

51. Community Foundation for Southeastern Michigan, *www.comnet.org/ local/orgs/comfound/respub/diversit/pat5.htm.*

52. The University of Buffalo has a Poland in the Classroom website that has many resources. The Matt Urban story can be accessed at *http://wings. buffalo.edu/info-poland/classroom/urban/story.*

53. Maisel, "The Poles Among Us," 6; see also Lopata, *Polish Americans,* 135; and Wytrwal, *Behold! The Polish Americans,* 228.

54. Ron Dzwonkowski, "It's Time to Pardon Pvt. Eddie Slovik," *Detroit Free Press,* 27 May 2001, E, 2.

55. Anthony R. Kosnik, "Their Votes Count," *The Eagle,* 1951. Unpublished high school yearbook for the semi-quincentennial of Orchard Lake St. Mary's High School; see also "Poles in Michigan," 29.

56. Kosnik, "Their Votes Count," 29–30.

57. Chrobot, "Poles," 221; see also Kosnik, "Their Votes Count," 30.

58. Wytrwal, *The Polish Experience in Detroit,* 231–2.

59. Interview with Judge David Szymanski, Wayne County Probate Court, 7 June 2001. I am indebted to Judge Szymanski for his interview and the many e-mails we exchanged in discussing his parents.

60. Maisel, "The Poles Among Us," 4.

61. Jerry Green, "Playing for Lions is a Family Affair," *Detroit News,* 4 May 2000, sec. F, 1,5.

62. Nat Fleischer and Sam Andre, *An Illustrated History of Boxing,* 5th ed. (Secaucus: Citadel Press, 1997), 219–20.

63. Interviews with Paul Paruk, Judge on the 31st District Court and chairman of the National Polish-American Sports Hall of Fame and Museum, 3, 5 June 2001.

For Further Reference

Libraries, Archives, and Museums

American Council for Polish Culture, *www.polishcultureacpc.org*

The Bentley Historical Library, University of Michigan, 1105 Beal Ave., Ann Arbor, MI 48109; Tel. (734) 764-3482; *www.umich.edu/~bhl/*

Burton Historical Collection, Detroit Public Library, 5201 Woodward Avenue, Detroit, MI 48202; Tel. (313) 833-1480

Calumet and Hecla Library, 101 Red Jacket Rd., Calumet, MI 49913, (906) 337-1976

Center for Polish Studies and Culture, Orchard Lake, MI 48324

Friends of Polish Art, 18156 Locherbie Rd., Birmingham, MI 48009: (313) 642-6991

Immigration History Research Center, University of Minnesota, 311 Andersen Library, 222 21st Ave. S, Minneapolis, MN 55455, Tel. (612) 625-4800

The Library of Michigan, Genealogy and Local History Collection, Michigan Library and Historical Center, 717 W. Allegan St., P.O. box 30007, Lansing, MI 48909; Tel. (517) 373-1300; *www.libofmich.lib.mi.us*

Madonna University, 36600 Schoolcraft Rd., Livonia, MI 48150: (313) 591-5000 The home of the Felician Sisters.

The North American Study Center for Polish Affairs, P.O. Box 7392, Ann Arbor, MI 48107

Polish American Historical Association c/o St. Mary's College, 3535 Indian Trail, Orchard Lake, MI 48324; Tel. (248) 683-1743 Polish Archives at same location

St. Charles Coalminer's Museum, St. Charles, MI 48655

State Archives of Michigan, Michigan Library and Historical Center, 717 W. Allegan St., Lansing, MI 48918; Tel. (517) 373-1408; *www.sos.state.mi.us/history/archive*

Books

Bukowczyk, John. *And My Children Did Not Know Me: A History of the Polish Americans.* Bloomington: Indiana University Press, 1987.

Dolan, Sean. *The Polish Americans (Immigrant Experience).* New York: Chelsea House Publishers, 1996.

Greene, Victor. *For God and Country: The Rise of Polish and Lithuanian Consciousness in America 1860–1910.* Madison: State Historical Society of Wisconsin, 1975.

Kuniczak, W.S. *My Name is Million.* New York: Doubleday & Co., 1978.

Kuniczak, W.S. *My Name is Million: An Illustrated History of the Poles in America.* New York: Hippocrene Books, 1999.

Lieberson, Stanley and Mary C. Waters. *From Many Strands: Ethnic and Racial Groups in Contemporary America.* New York: Russell Sage Foundation, 1988.

Lukas, Richard C. *The Forgotten Holocaust: The Poles Under German Occupation 1939–1944.* Lexington: University Press of Kentucky, 1986.

Obidinski, Eugene and Helen Stankiewicz Zand. *Polish Folkways in America: Community and Family.* New York: Lanham, 1987.

Pienkos, Donald. *For Your Freedom Through Ours: Polish American Efforts on Poland's Behalf 1863–1991.* Boulder: East European Monographs (New York: Columbia University Press, U.S. distributor), 1992.

Polzin, Theresita. *The Polish Americans Whence and Whither.* Pulaski, Wisconsin: Franciscan Publishers, 1973.

Steven, Stewart. *The Poles.* New York: Macmillan, 1982.

Tec, Nechama. *When Light Pierced the Darkness: Christian Rescue of Jews in Nazi-Occupied Poland.* New York: Oxford University Press, 1986.

Vraniak, John M. *The Polish Trivia Book.* Hamtramck: Avenue Publishing Co., 1991.

Media Organizations

Dziennek Polski, 12021 Joseph Campau, Hamtramck, MI 48212: (313) 365-1990

Polish Daily News, 1960 Van Dyke, Detroit, MI 48234: (313) 366-4900

Polish Radio Mass, WNZK-AM 680/690, 21700 Northwestern Hwy., Southfield,
MI 48076, (313) 557-3500

Polish Village, WNZK-AM 680/690, 2100 Woodward Ave. #212, Royal Oak, MI
48073; (313-548-2524

Polka News, P.O. Box 57, St. Charles, MI 48655 (517) 865-6710

Swiat Polski, 11903 Joseph Campau, Hamtramck, MI 48212; (313) 365-1990.

Polish American Radio Network, 4634 Jonathan St. Dearborn, MI 48126; (313)
945-0666

Polish World, 11903 Joseph Campau, Hamtramck, MI 48212; (313) 365-1990

Arts Organizations

Art of Poland Associates, 240 Chesterfield Rd., Bloomfield Hills, MI 48013; (248)
642-2730

Bal Polonais, 240 Chesterfield Rd., Bloomfield Hills, MI 48013; (248) 642-2730

Gwiazda Dancers, P.R.C.U. Hall, 2314 Caniff, Hamtramck, MI 48212, (313) 365-
6942

Halka Dancers, Our Lady Queen of Heaven Church, 8175 E. Lantz, Detroit, MI
48234; (313) 891-2403

Lutnia Singing Society, 9711 Conant, Hamtramck, MI 48212; (313) 526-3375

Mala Polska Folk Dancers, American Polish Cultural Center, 2975 E. Maple Rd.,
Troy, MI 48083; (810) 939-2226

Polish Art Center, 9539 Joseph Campau, Hamtramck, MI 48212; (313) 874-2242;
www.polartcenter.com

Pope John Paul II Dance Ensemble, St. Anne's Parish, 32000 Mound Rd., Warren,
MI 48092; (313) 268-3780

Rzeszow Dancers, 8136 Bernice, Centerline, MI 48015

Tatry Dancers, 26123 McDonald, Dearborn, MI 48125; (313) 274-0183

Index